BATS SET I

SPEAR-NOSED BATS

Tamara L. Britton
ABDO Publishing Company

visit us at
www.abdopublishing.com

Published by ABDO Publishing Company, 8000 West 78th Street, Edina, Minnesota 55439. Copyright © 2011 by Abdo Consulting Group, Inc. International copyrights reserved in all countries. No part of this book may be reproduced in any form without written permission from the publisher. The Checkerboard Library™ is a trademark and logo of ABDO Publishing Company.

Printed in the United States of America, North Mankato, Minnesota.
042010
092010

Cover Photo: © Merlin D. Tuttle, Bat Conservation International, www.batcon.org
Interior Photos: Animals Animals p. 5; Getty Images pp. 17, 19, 21;
    © Merlin D. Tuttle, Bat Conservation International, www.batcon.org p. 9;
    Peter Arnold p. 13; Photolibrary p. 11

Editor: Heidi M.D. Elston
Art Direction & Cover Design: Neil Klinepier

Library of Congress Cataloging-in-Publication Data

Britton, Tamara L., 1963-
  Spear-nosed bats / Tamara L. Britton.
     p. cm. -- (Bats)
  Includes index.
  ISBN 978-1-61613-393-1
  1. Phyllostomus--Juvenile literature. I. Title.
  QL737.C57B748 2011
  599.4'5--dc22
                              2010009934

CONTENTS

SPEAR-NOSED BATS

There are more than 1,100 species of bats in the world. Seven species in the family **Phyllostomidae** are spear-nosed bats. As the name suggests, they have a nose with a pointed leaf. This long flap of skin looks like the sharp head of a spear!

Bats are mammals. One-quarter of all mammals are bats. Like other mammals, bats have hair. And, mother bats give birth to live babies and feed them with milk. Yet bats can do something no other mammal can do. Bats can fly!

Some people are afraid of bats. It is true that some bats can carry disease. Yet bats are also

helpful. Each year, insect-eating bats consume millions of insect pests. Bats that eat fruits and flowers help plants reproduce. These useful creatures are an important part of their ecosystem.

Spear-nosed bats are part of a group of bats known as leaf-nosed bats.

Where They're Found

Bats are found all over the world. These adaptable creatures live everywhere except the polar regions and a few ocean islands.

Spear-nosed bats occupy **tropical** and **subtropical** climates. They can be found in many regions in North, Central, and South America. They live from southern Mexico to Belize and Guatemala. From there, their range extends south to Brazil, Paraguay, and Argentina. Spear-nosed bats have also been found on the island of Trinidad.

Spear-nosed bats prefer to live in **humid** places. They occupy a wide variety of **habitats**. They can be found in both forests and open areas.

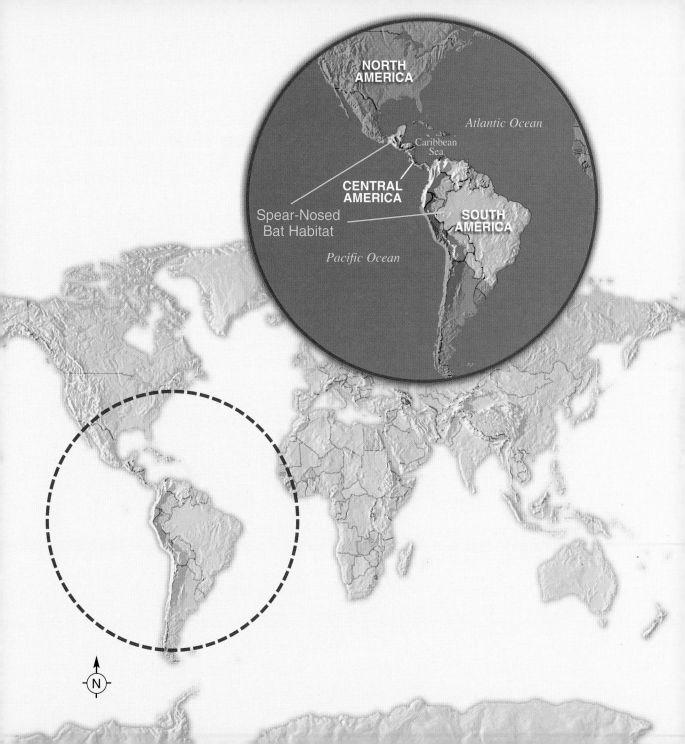

NORTH
AMERICA

Atlantic Ocean

Caribbean
Sea

CENTRAL
AMERICA

Spear-Nosed
Bat Habitat

SOUTH
AMERICA

Pacific Ocean

N

WHERE THEY LIVE

Spear-nosed bats are **nocturnal**. At night, they swoop through the air. They spend their days **roosting** in hidden places. Caves, **culverts**, hollow trees, and buildings are favorite resting spots for spear-nosed bats.

A spear-nosed bat roosts by hanging upside down by its feet. Each foot has five toes. Each of the toes has a sharp, curved claw. To roost, the bat grabs onto a roosting surface with its claws. As the bat relaxes, a **tendon** in each foot closes the claws on the roosting site.

Different species of spear-nosed bats have different roosting habits. Some spear-nosed bats like to **roost** alone. Others roost in small groups of two to four bats.

Still other spear-nosed bats roost in colonies. Each colony consists of one male and several females. The bats in a colony can stay together for many years.

A colony of spear-nosed bats roosts comfortably in a cave.

SIZES

The spear-nosed bat is a medium-sized bat. Together, its head and body measure 2 to 4 inches (5 to 10 cm) long. A tail adds 0.25 to 1 inch (1 to 2.5 cm) to that length. The bat's arms are about 1.9 to 3.75 inches (4.8 to 9.5 cm) long. Its **wingspan** is about 18 inches (46 cm).

In comparison, some bats are much bigger than spear-nosed bats. The Malayan flying fox is the world's largest bat. It can grow more than 16 inches (40 cm) long. This impressive bat weighs about 2 to 3.5 pounds (1 to 1.5 kg). Its wingspan reaches an amazing 5 feet (1.5 m) or more!

A spear-nosed bat's short wings help it fly in close quarters, such as a cave.

Other bats are tinier than spear-nosed bats. Kitti's hog-nosed bats grow to only 1 inch (2.5 cm) long. That is about the size of a large bumblebee! Although their bodies are small, their **wingspan** is 6 inches (15 cm).

SHAPES

Spear-nosed bats have strong bodies and wings. Their eyes are small. This makes their spearhead-shaped nose leaf very obvious! The tips of their large ears can be round or pointed. Small, wartlike bumps surround their grooved chins. They have shorter tails than some bats.

Some spear-nosed bat species have short, soft fur. Others have fur that is long and woolly. Among the different species the fur can be dark brown, chestnut brown, light gray, or red. A bat's undersides are a lighter shade than its body color.

Spear-nosed bats have two arms. Each arm has a hand with four fingers and a thumb. The thumb has a claw that helps the bat grab onto surfaces.

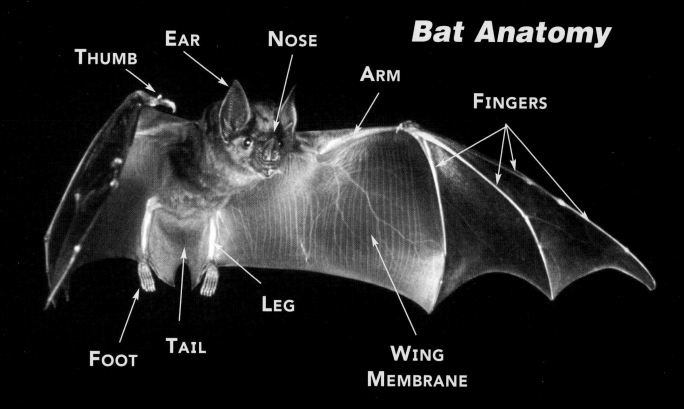

THUMB EAR NOSE **Bat Anatomy**

ARM

FINGERS

LEG

FOOT TAIL

WING
MEMBRANE

The wings are black, elastic **membranes**. They
stretch between the bat's fingers, body, and legs. A
spear-nosed bat's wings also connect its legs and
tail. This forms a tail pouch.

SENSES

To move around in the dark, a spear-nosed bat uses echolocation. This is a simple process. The spear-nosed bat makes high-pitched sounds from its throat or its nose. These sounds go out and bounce off objects such as trees, buildings, or insects.

The sounds return to the bat as echoes. They tell the bat the size and location of the objects. The spear-nosed bat uses this information to fly safely, find food, and avoid danger.

Some scholars believe the leaf on the spear-nosed bat's nose helps it with echolocation. Some spear-nosed bat species are very **accurate** with their echolocation. They can locate an object to within 0.06 inches (0.4 cm)!

Sound wave sent out by bat

Echo wave received by bat

DEFENSE

Since spear-nosed bats are **nocturnal**, they fly around at night. They avoid many predators that hunt during the day.

However, spear-nosed bats still face predators. Snakes hide near cave entrances and grab bats from the air. Cats, dogs, raccoons, and skunks prowl the night looking for a tasty meal. Birds of prey are other threats. If a bat becomes caught in a large spider's web, the spider may eat it. And, some bats eat other bats!

Sometimes, the bat can escape danger by flying away. It may also avoid predators by hiding. The dark color of a spear-nosed bat's fur makes it hard for predators to see it at night. And during the day, the bats choose dark places in which to safely **roost**.

Spear-nosed bats eat other bats, such as short-tailed leaf-nosed bats.

FOOD

Spear-nosed bats also need to eat. So, they are also predators. Their prey tries to avoid them, too!

Spear-nosed bat species eat a variety of foods. Some eat fruits. They also eat insects. Sometimes, spear-nosed bats will eat small animals such as mice and lizards. And, they even eat smaller bats!

In the evening, spear-nosed bats leave their **roosting** sites to hunt for food. They fly to feeding sites up to two miles (3.25 km) away.

Some spear-nosed bats will do something few other bats will do. They share food with other members of their colony! They will call to other bats to alert them to the food source.

Lizards must watch out for hungry spear-nosed bats!

BABIES

Spear-nosed bats mate once a year. In colonial species, the colony's male usually fathers all the babies in that group. But during mating time, other young male bats may challenge him. He will need to successfully defend his colony in order to breed with its females.

After mating, a female spear-nosed bat has one baby in April or May. The baby bat is called a pup. A spear-nosed pup weighs about 0.5 ounces (13 g).

When a pup is born, it climbs onto its mother's chest and begins nursing. For the first several days, the mother takes her pup with her when she goes out hunting. When the pup is older, she leaves it at the **roost**.

This spear-nosed bat has returned to the roost covered with pollen! Her pup is nursing under her left wing.

The pup begins flying around its **roost** at about six weeks old. When it is two months old, the young bat strikes out on its own. It will join a new community and mate. The spear-nosed bat will then have pups of its own and take its place in its ecosystem.

GLOSSARY

accurate - free of errors.

culvert - a drain for water crossing under a road, a sidewalk, or a railroad.

habitat - a place where a living thing is naturally found.

humid - damp or moist, especially relating to air.

membrane - a thin, easily bent layer of animal tissue.

nocturnal - active at night.

Phyllostomidae (fihl-uh-STOH-mih-dee) - the scientific name for a family of New World leaf-nosed bats.

roost - to perch or settle down to rest. A roost is a place, such as a cave or a tree, where animals rest.

subtropical - relating to an area bordering a tropical area. A tropical area has a climate in which there is no frost and plants can grow all year long.

tendon - a band of tough fibers that joins a muscle to another body part, such as a bone.

tropical - having a climate in which there is no frost and plants can grow all year long.

wingspan - the distance from one wing tip to the other when the wings are spread.

WEB SITES

To learn more about spear-nosed bats, visit ABDO Publishing Company on the World Wide Web at **www.abdopublishing.com**. Web sites about spear-nosed bats are featured on our Book Links page. These links are routinely monitored and updated to provide the most current information available.

INDEX